Gentle Breeze

Finding Comfort, Hope, and Purpose
in the Midst of Your Storm

Joan M. Blake

Key to Life
PUBLISHING COMPANY

Copyright © 2019 by Joan M. Blake • All rights reserved.

No part of this publication may be reproduced in any form or by any means, electronic or mechanical, including photocopy, recording, or any information or retrieval system, without written permission from the author.

ISBN 978-0-9814609-6-3

Published by
Key to Life Publishing Company • P.O. Box 190971 • Boston, MA 02119
keytolifepublishingcompany.com

Unless otherwise indicated, Scriptures are taken from the Holy Bible, *New International Version*® (NIV®): Copyright ©1973, 1978, 1984, 2011 by Biblica, Inc.®, 1820 Jet Stream Drive, Colorado Springs, CO 80921. Used by permission. All rights reserved worldwide.

Scriptures taken from the *New King James Version*®: Copyright © 1982 by Thomas Nelson Bibles, P.O. Box 141000, Nashville, TN 37214. Used by permission. All rights reserved.

Scriptures taken from *The Living Bible:* Copyright © 1971 by Tyndale House Foundation. Used by permission of Tyndale House Publishers Inc., 351 Executive Drive, Carol Stream, IL 60188. All rights reserved.

Dedication

I dedicate this book to our daughter, Jo-An. I thank God, and will always be grateful to Him, for giving me the strength, determination, and opportunity to help our daughter, and for transforming me into a patient, loving, kind parent.

Acknowledgement

I thank my husband, Carl, who took care of our household while I spent hours working on this manuscript. I thank my sons and my daughters: Anthony, Rese, Monique and Jo-An, for their continued love and encouragement. I am grateful for the support I receive from my prayer partners, friends, and extended family.

I thank God for his love, peace, strength, wisdom and insights he gave me during all phases of writing this book. I am convinced, that in him, I move and have my being. (Acts 17:28) I know that there is nothing too hard for God to do in your life or in mine. We must "be strong in the Lord and in his mighty power." (Ephesians 6:10) We must take refuge in Him. The Scripture states, "As for God, his way is perfect: The LORD'S word is flawless; he shields all who take refuge in him."

—*2 Samuel 22:31*

Introduction

I have experienced tremendous ups and downs caring for my special-needs daughter. While I do not question God about my trials, I do feel overwhelmed and drained every single day from the toil of helping her to realize the importance of getting up and getting ready for the day God has made.

However, I do not feel alone. For the Holy Spirit is always there, helping me, encouraging me, keeping me and walking with me. When I feel like giving up, the Holy Spirit reminds me, that I have succeeded in everything God has put before me, only with the Spirit's guidance, strength, wisdom and understanding. Knowing that God allows me to go through difficulties for His divine will and for His glory has been comforting to me.

Gentle Breeze: Finding Comfort, Hope, and Purpose in the Midst of Your Storm metaphorically depicts the wind of the Holy Spirit. I want to convey to the reader how I feel throughout my journey and explain the depths of the Holy Spirit's reach in bringing me out of my distresses.

Parents who are going through crises, who feel alone in their journeys, or who feel overwhelmed by the tasks of caring for their special-needs children will find this book helpful. This devotional includes 31 short chapters; each highlights a scriptural reference, a discussion of the issue, and a place for the reader to reflect and answer related questions.

I pray that, as you read this book, you will receive the Holy Spirit's guidance, and the strength and zeal to enable you to overcome your difficulties. May God be praised. May God be with you.

Table of Contents

Introduction V

1. You Are Carrying Me 3
2. I Hear Your Soft Whisper 5
3. You Restore Me 7
4. You Lead Me to My Destination 9
5. You Calm My Fears 11
6. You Protect Me 13
7. You Give Me Life and Peace 15
8. You Guide Me to the Light of Your Love 17
9. You Bring Things to My Remembrance 19
10. I Keep in Step with You 21
11. You Remove My Fears of the Unknown 23
12. You Uproot the Burdens I Carry 25
13. You Give Me Hope 27
14. You Take Away Anxiety 29
15. You Will Never Leave or Forsake Me 31
16. You Empower Me 33
17. You Allow Me to Be in the Fire of Affliction 35
18. My Gifts Will Be Realized 37

19	You Are Fashioning Me	39
20	I Feel Tension	41
21	In the Stillness	43
22	Who Am I?	45
23	I Will Go Where You Send Me	47
24	I Can Live Again	49
25	You Love Me Unconditionally	51
26	You Conquer My Storms	53
27	You Give Me Strength and Joy	55
28	You Give Me Freedom	57
29	You Touch Me	59
30	I Cannot See from a Distance	61
31	You Tear Down the Barriers	63

About the Author ... 65

Photo Credits ... 66

You Are Carrying Me

He tends his flock like a shepherd: He gathers the lambs in his arms and carries them close to his heart; He gently leads those that have young.

—Isaiah 40:11

As you hover over me, I feel your touch, but I cannot see you. I forget that you are there for me, washing away the debris—the worries, the aches, the pains, and the scales. I continue to bathe in disbelief, unable to fathom that you are with me, carrying me, holding me, comforting me, helping me, supporting me, and making a way out of no way for me. I desire to soak in your glory as I strive to be me.

Reflection

Explain a difficult time in your life-journey in which the Holy Spirit, a good friend or a stranger was carrying you, helping you, supporting you, and making a way out for you.

I Hear Your Soft Whisper

My sheep hear My voice, and I know them, and they follow Me.
—John 10:27 NKJV

You lift me from the bottomless pit and put my feet on solid ground. Although I cannot see it, I know it, for I feel your presence and hear your whispers. I hear your whispers amid your gentleness and kindness. Your soft whispers quietly and swiftly penetrate through thoughts weaved in my mind and bring my thoughts captive to the obedience of Christ. ❀

Reflection
Have you ever heard a soft whisper guiding you at a time when you were experiencing difficulties? How did you respond?

You Restore Me

He restores my soul; He leads me in the paths of righteousness for His name's sake.

—Psalm 23:3 NKJV

You restore me from the weariness of the heat and storms. Your Gentle Breeze penetrates my inner spirit, and my body is restored to health. You restore me to the person you first created—a daughter/son of the Almighty God, one on whom God has put His seal. You complete my restoration process as you remake all of my broken parts and glue them together according to their originality.

Reflection

Explain a time in your life when you felt broken but were restored in both mind and body.

You Lead Me to My Destination

He makes me to lie down in green pastures; He leads me beside the still waters.
—*Psalm 23:2 NKJV*

You lead me as I journey from one place to another or from one position to another. You act so gently, so swiftly, so peaceably, so uniquely, that I do not know when or how you do it. When you move me, you redefine me; you dissuade me from looking at myself the way people look at me. You see me at my greatest potential. You see me for who I am, not who I was, but who you made me to become. And you are leading me to my destination.

Reflection
Explain how you have been redefined at any point in your life-journey.

You Calm My Fears

He calms the storm, so that its waves are still.
—Psalm 107:29 NKJV

In difficult situations, I feel calm, because you are surrounding me with your wind of peace. You are holding me tightly in your arms, which helps me feel secure and safe from harm. When you are holding me close to your bosom, I feel your heart against mine, beating with a slow, consistent rhythm that lets me know I have no reason to be afraid, for I am under your authority, and you pre-ordained my life before the foundation of the world. Gentle Breeze, you are never in a hurry, and you want me to live my life slowly, steadily, and focused.

Reflection

Explain a difficult situation you have encountered and how you were able to maintain calmness in that situation.

You Protect Me

He will shield you with his wings! They will shelter you. His faithful promises are your armor.
—Psalm 91:4 TLB

You protect me from the burning, scorching sun. I feel no burns, pains or scars, because you provide a protective shield over my entire body. You shield me from the hurts and pains others have caused me, and I no longer feel disappointed or shattered by their aftermath. ❀

Reflection

Explain how you have or have not overcome the hurts and pains others have caused you. If you are still hurting, how do you plan to deal with the pain?

You Give Me Life and Peace

These things I have spoken to you, that in Me you may have peace. In the world you will have tribulation; but be of good cheer, I have overcome the world.
—John 16:33 NKJV

Your wind is strong; it takes me to the water-brooks, where I sit and gaze at the expanse of water you created. And I realize that, when I drink from the water of life, I can never be thirsty, for I drink of your Spirit, who gives life.

You take away worries and anxieties from me and fill my soul and my mind with peace. Your peace energizes me and lifts me from the bondage of decay to a life filled with dreams and endless possibilities that you plan for me. Your peace gives me a taste of what heaven is like—walking on the streets of gold, praising, worshiping and thanking you all day long, with nothing on my mind, except you.

Reflection
Explain how you feel energized by life and peace.

You Guide Me to the Light of Your Love

Then Jesus spoke to them again, saying, "I am the light of the world. He who follows Me shall not walk in darkness but have the light of life."
—John 8:12 NKJV

I picture myself skipping and jumping, as I feel your Gentle Breeze penetrating the very hairs of my head that you have numbered. I look up to the blue skies shining their lights of beauty, and I remember that you are light, and that no darkness can overcome your light. Thank you for guiding me to the light of your love.

Reflection

What comes to mind when you observe blue skies? How do you explain light and darkness?

You Bring Things to My Remembrance

So he said to me, "This is the word of the Lord to Zerubbabel: 'Not by might nor by power, but by my Spirit' says the Lord Almighty."
—Zechariah 4:6

You remind me that it is by your gentle spirit, and not by my power or by my might, that I achieve anything. You bring things to my remembrance when I walk beside you, hand in hand, and learn of your will for my life.

I can now turn a new page in my life-journey, having understood that you have sought me and have found me, and that you satisfy my longing heart. I am with you, and you are with me. I long to hear your secrets, Gentle Breeze.

Reflection

Has there been a point in your life when you needed help in making a major decision but decided to make it on your own? Explain the outcome and what you would have done differently if given another chance.

I Keep in Step with You

The steps of good men are directed by the Lord. He delights in each step they take.
—Psalm 37:23 TLB

As I go through valleys and hills, I keep in step with you, because you know the bumps and stumbling blocks I will encounter. You have taught me to persevere, and not to look back, regardless of the rough terrain I face, for you will make a smooth path for me.

Reflection

Some people persevere and overcome stumbling blocks, while others keep looking back and cannot move beyond their past. Explain a difficult stumbling block in your life and the steps you took to deal with it.

You Remove My Fears of the Unknown

Truly I tell you, if anyone says to this mountain, "Go, throw yourself into the sea," and does not doubt in their heart but believes that what they say will happen, it will be done for them.
—Mark 11:23

You removed fears of the unknown that were embedded in my mind and you have not chastised me for the way I felt. Because you are the beginning and the ending and know all about me, You have shown me that I have no reason to fear the unknown, for you will continue to care for me. My fears are now gone, for your wind has blown them away.

Reflection
What fears seem to linger in your mind? How do you intend to respond to those fears?

You Uproot the Burdens I Carry

I removed his shoulder from the burden; His hands were freed from the baskets.
—Psalm 81:6 NKJV

You uproot burdens that hold me captive. You show me that my mind and heart can no longer make room for burdens, which weigh me down. You let me know that I am yours. You are there when I shed my tears, when I feel insignificant, when I cannot satisfy the longings of people, and when I will rather rest and depend totally on you. When I feel the urge to take on more than I can, you remind me that your yoke is easy, and your burden is light. *(Matthew 11:30)*

Reflection

What burdens are you carrying? How are you dealing with them?

You Give Me Hope

For you have been my hope, Sovereign Lord, my confidence since my youth.
—Psalm 71:5

I hear the rushing mighty wind, symbolic of your power and might, which moves me and changes my circumstances. Amid the sounds, I hear your still, soft voice encouraging me and giving me hope.

You pick me up when I feel sad and give me hope during challenging times. You hope in me without having undue expectations of me. You allow me to live freely, being patient and loving toward me. You fill my life with hope and faith so I can realize the things you have set before me. I no longer feel rejected, for your gentleness has given me confidence and composure.

Reflection

What emotions from your past seem to surface? For example, have you dealt with rejection, abandonment, fear, guilt, anger, or unforgiveness? Explain the reason(s) that cause certain emotions to linger from your past.

14 You Take Away Anxiety

Do not be anxious about anything, but in every situation, by prayer and petition, with thanksgiving, present your requests to God.
—Philippians 4:6

Sometimes I get anxious when I think about ways to share and to help others. You sweep away every anxious thought, leaving me with space to think and breathe. Your love dispels every desire to be anxious about my life. I strive to be all you have purposed me to be. You know how much I can do and how much you want me to do for your glory and for your kingdom. Your gentle love erases all anxiety from my mind. ❀

Reflection
Explain the circumstances that trigger anxiety. What methods have you used to deal with anxiety?

You Will Never Leave or Forsake Me

Be strong and courageous. Do not be afraid or terrified because of them, for the Lord your God goes with you; he will never leave you nor forsake you.
—Deuteronomy 31:6

I must tarry a little longer and wait until the appropriate time for you to unveil your secrets concerning me. I will hear your voice clearly and will obey your commands. You shatter my fears and allow me to rest with full assurance that you will never leave or forsake me. You care for me and consider every detail of my life. You blow me away with your gentle breeze of security. I am secured in you; I can rest in you during difficult times. You have been with me, sheltering me, helping me, and strengthening me. For these things, I am grateful.

Reflection
Explain why you feel insecure sometimes and what you need to do/think to feel more secure.

You Empower Me

Your word is a lamp for my feet, a light on my path.
—Psalm 119:105

You take me out of the miry clay and bring me to a safe place. I come to a river where I can drink pure water that is nourishing for my soul. I feel your Gentle Breeze as you pass by, and I hear you whispering in my ear, assuring me about my uniqueness and my usefulness and the plans you have for me. I also hear your sweet whispers of your love for me, and I see the place you have set aside in your heart for me.

Your word has empowered me to step out of my comfort zone with soundness of mind and to focus, by telling others of your redeeming power and love. You are my shield, and you have given me spiritual weaponry to protect and keep me. Wherever you send me, I will go. Whatever you want me to write, I will write. I am yours, Gentle Breeze; I am yours.

Reflection

Explain areas where you are: **a** unique, and **b** useful to family, job, community, and the world at large.

You Allow Me to Be in the Fire of Affliction

Behold, I have refined you, but not as silver; I have tested you in the furnace of affliction.
—Isaiah 48:10 NKJV

You allow me to be in the fire of affliction for your glory and for your purposes. I will not worry about the distractions that come my way. I will walk with you, for you have called me your daughter/son. You give me the words to say and show me the way out of my difficulties.

You teach me to be strong and to be of good courage, and I will continue to heed your words, which are life. I will trust you during times of testing, as you shape me into the person you want me to be, fit for use in your kingdom; for you are the potter, and I am the clay. I will not ascribe glory to myself; I will be humble and love all people, even if they have hurt me in the past. I will wait until I see your goodness manifesting in my life. You hold everything together; I will trust you and not despair. I will have hope, for I am your daughter/son. I know you will deliver me.

Reflection
Explain the ways you have dealt with difficult times in your life. What have you learned from those times?

My Gifts Will Be Realized

We have different gifts, according to the grace given to each of us. If your gift is prophesying, then prophesy in accordance with your faith.
—Romans 12:6

I trust you, Gentle Breeze. You are the wind; you orchestrate the wind. You know where the wind blows, you know how strong it blows, and you know when it should blow in my life. You help me to understand that you will chart the course of my life and I will respond with trust.

I understand that my weariness is not a part of your plan. For you have delivered me from weariness, helplessness and hopelessness, where the enemy wants to keep me. Instead, you have given me zeal. You have freed my mind from the enemy's plans and given me rest to believe, Gentle Breeze, that you are moving me to a place where my gifts will be realized. ❊

Reflection
Everyone has gifts, whether or not you realize this. Describe yours.

You Are Fashioning Me

Your hands have made me and fashioned me; Give me understanding, that I may learn Your commandments.
—Psalm 119:73 NKJV

You are taking me to a place of knowledge to understand who I am. I am yours, and you are mine. You touch me with your divine inspiration as you propel me to greater heights in you. You help me to understand that the things I am going through are intended to fashion and mold me into a vessel fit for use in God's kingdom. But I look at my difficult circumstances and forget that you use these tests to shape my character. Thank you for fashioning me.

Reflection

Do you agree that the difficulties you and I experience are only tests that shape our character or increase our strength? Explain how your difficulties and/or tests have shaped or are shaping your character.

I Feel Tension

They will be like a tree planted by the water that sends out its roots by the stream. It does not fear when heat comes; its leaves are always green. It has no worries in a year of drought and never fails to bear fruit.
—Jeremiah 17:8

I feel tension in my neck and shoulders from the stress of life, but your Gentle Breeze allows me to breathe fresh air so I can dispel the tension. You remind me of your beautiful creation, including the sun, moon, lands and seas, surrounded by beautiful flowers and trees, swaying and being nurtured from your Gentle Breeze. Some of the trees and flowers respond favorably to their natural habitat, losing their petals and leaves in the winter and regaining them in the spring. I need to look forward to another season in which my life can be meaningful and purposeful, as your creation.

Reflection

Where do you feel tension, and why? Consider two examples from God's creation, and discuss how they react (e.g., trees swaying in the wind, waves breaking against rocks). Based on your insights from them, how should you react to life?

In the Stillness

He says, "Be still, and know that I am God; I will be exalted among the nations, I will be exalted in the earth."
—Psalm 46:10

Being still is an act of submission, which allows me to listen and think. In the stillness, I feel your strength, your power, and your authority; because when I am still, you blow me to your direction, your purpose, and your will.

- In the stillness, I let go of my anxiety, my fears and my ill thoughts.
- In the stillness, you carry me.
- In the stillness, you remind me of my position as your daughter/son.
- In the stillness, you calm me.
- In the stillness, you elevate me and show me how far you have brought me.

You do all of this because you are Gentle Breeze.

Reflection

Practice being still for 15 minutes or more first thing in the morning or just before going to bed. Explain your responses.

Who Am I?

22

See what great love the Father has lavished on us, that we should be called children of God! And that is what we are! The reason the world does not know us is that it did not know him.

—I John 3:1

- You allow me to know who I am in you.
- I am your creation, because the great "I AM" created me.
- I am the head, not the tail.
- I am led by you.
- I am blessed to be a blessing.
- I am secured, because "I AM" sacrificed for me.
- I am created for good works.
- I am yours, and you are mine.
- I am never alone, for you are forever at my side.
- I am loved by you.
- I am forgiven.
- I am healed.
- I am favored wherever I go.
- I am gifted.
- I am an heir/heiress.
- I am kind.
- I am good and generous.
- I am filled with joy.
- I am made in the image and likeliness of my Heavenly Father.
- I am justified.
- I am a laborer for the kingdom of God.

- I am motivated for good works.
- I am organized and focused.
- I am an overcomer.
- I am precious.
- I am redeemed.
- I am transformed.
- I am set free.
- I am victorious.
- I am a winner.
- I am zealous for the things of the Kingdom.

Reflection

Create and add a list of who you are to the above. What is significant to you, and why?

I Will Go Where You Send Me

Then I heard the voice of the Lord saying, "Whom shall I send? And who will go for us?" And I said, "Here am I. Send me!"
—Isaiah 6:8

I emerge as a new person with soundness of mind and focus, because Your word has empowered me. You position me as your daughter/son and give me the mantle to be your witness, to share with countless others regarding your unconditional love for them. You are my shield and have given me spiritual weaponry to protect and keep me.

I will go wherever your Gentle Breeze blows me, for you lead and guide me. When I follow you, the wind, I cannot go wrong, because the sound comes from heaven. I cannot see the wind, but I hear a strong, buzzing wind with a forceful noise, and I feel you tenderly carrying me to my destination. I feel your touch on my shoulders beckoning me to follow you. I will go where you send me and write under your direction and inspiration. ✿

Reflection
Who do you believe you are destined to be? What are you destined to do? Give reasons for both.

I Can Live Again

Then he said to me, "Prophesy to these bones and say to them, 'Dry bones, hear the word of the Lord!'" This is what the Sovereign Lord says to these bones: I will make breath enter you, and you will come to life.
—Ezekiel 37:4-5

Recently I was in the valley, but you heard my cries, and you brought me up again to meaningful heights—to a place where the evil one could not take me down. You tested me to see if I would doubt your faithfulness, but you delivered me. You brought me up from the muck and miry clay and carried me to a place of safety so I could think again, breathe again, hope again, wish again, and live again.

Now, I am returning in rest, assured that beneath me are not harsh weeds or painful tares, but living water from which I can drink, and which brings refreshing life to my body, soul and spirit. My body is immersed in wholeness, my mind freed up, and my soul renewed. I feel stirred, as I am regenerated—traveling to places where your Gentle Breeze has directed me, to people and things. As I continue to drink living water, my thought patterns change, and I gain strength. I have peace and serenity. I feel fulfilled and energized, and I have purpose. ❦

Reflection
Describe a low point you had arrived in your life-journey and the steps you took to enable yourself to live again. What did you learn from that period in your life?

You Love Me Unconditionally

Hatred stirs up conflict, but love covers over all wrongs.
—Proverbs 10:12

Your loving hands are constantly at work in my life as I let go and let you handle the things that trouble me, such as my burdens, my needs, and my wants. You show me unconditional love by listening to my call for help. You respond by gently leading me through dark waters.

The wind of love is approaching me, passing me by. I cannot hold back the love I inherited from you. Because you love me, I must love others. I must love even when I do not feel like it, when others have hurt me, when they do not understand me, or when they refuse to show me they care. The wind of love you pour into me makes it possible to love others as you love me.

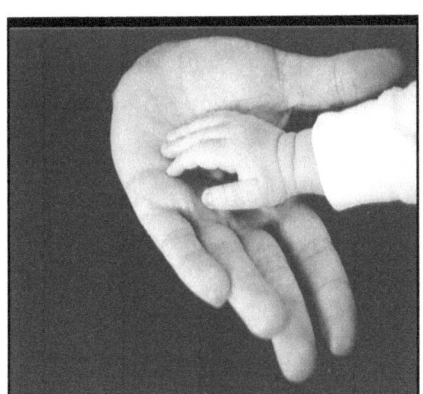

Reflection

Explain your position on, "Why you should love others, even when they have hurt you." Give an example where you have applied the above.

You Conquer My Storms

Then he got into the boat and his disciples followed him. Suddenly a furious storm came up on the lake, so that the waves swept over the boat. But Jesus was sleeping. The disciples went and woke him, saying, "Lord, save us! We're going to drown!" He replied, "You of little faith, why are you so afraid?" Then he got up and rebuked the winds and the waves, and it was completely calm.

—Matthew 8:23-26

Your gentleness helps me conquer and overcome the storms that seem to overtake me. You bring quietness to my restless soul and strength to my weak body, by helping me discern future storms coming my way. Your wind tears down unkind words, unfit relationships, ungrateful people, and things that are not good for me. The wind of your spirit repositions me and helps me focus.

Reflection

How do you handle stresses of life—for example, a separation, a divorce, a loved one who is ill, or a family member, close friend or co-worker turning against you?

You Give Me Strength and Joy

The LORD is my strength and my shield; my heart trusts in him, and he helps me. My heart leaps for joy, and with my song I praise him.
—Psalm 28:7

You give me strength for the mission you have set before me. You let me know that I can do all things, because you pour strength into my weak limbs. You give me joy as I feel the wind of your presence: motivating me, loving me, energizing me, and saturating me. Your presence lets me know that, regardless of the turbulence I experience, I have joy in knowing that you are with me and will never leave or forsake me.

Reflection
How do you maintain strength and joy in your life?

You Give Me Freedom

But now that you have been set free from sin and have become slaves of God, the benefit you reap leads to holiness, and the result is eternal life.
—Romans 6:22

I recognize the freedom you have given me as I move to and fro. You guide me by the wind of your presence, and by your kind and pleasant touch. I know I am free, for I feel like a little girl again, sometimes skipping my jump-rope or walking through the woods to find my favorite butterfly. I picture myself as that butterfly that has gone through many changes and become that beautiful monarch of different colors. What freedom you gave that butterfly! What freedom you gave me!

Reflection

Is someone or something holding you back from exercising your freedom? Explain what you need to do to regain your freedom.

You Touch Me

Then the Lord put forth His hand and touched my mouth, and the Lord said to me: "Behold, I have put My words in your mouth."
—Jeremiah 1:9 NKJV

Wherever I go or whatever I do, your Gentle Breeze touches me, and I know all is well. When you touch me, you implant life-changing thoughts on my heart and leave lasting impressions of fervor on my life. You give me hope when I realize you are there, you are real, and you are mine. You let me know it is the condition of my heart that perpetuates the need for me to move forward with passion and compassion.

Reflection

Describe the state of your heart. Do you have a loving heart for people? How do you operate in life with passion (zeal) and compassion (mercy)? If you do not operate with passion and compassion, explain what you must do to begin to do so.

I Cannot See from a Distance

But when he, the Spirit of truth, comes, he will guide you into all the truth. He will not speak on his own; he will speak only what he hears, and he will tell you what is yet to come.
—John 16:13

Although I cannot see from a distance, I understand where you are taking me. Weariness, anxiety, and strongholds block the path to my destiny, but I refuse to give up. I will follow you wherever you take me, for you are my guide.

Reflection
Describe your weaknesses or issues that have prevented you from reaching your purpose.

You Tear Down the Barriers

The weapons we fight with are not the weapons of the world.
On the contrary, they have divine power to demolish strongholds.
—II Corinthians 10:4

You reach down with your gentle hand and tear down the barriers that have kept me trapped for so long. You allow me to inhale the freshness and coolness of the wind penetrating my mind and body as you break through the walls of suffocation and oppression that have tried to overtake me. You allow me to walk this earth by gently carrying me. Thank you, Gentle Breeze.

Reflection

List and describe at least two barriers that have kept you from realizing your success and/or freedom.

About the Author

Joan M. Blake is a motivational speaker and spiritual-life coach. She is the author of six inspirational books, including, *Standing on His Promises: Finding Comfort, Hope, and Purpose in the Midst of Your Storm,* published by Key to Life Publishing Company. She conducts women's retreats, workshops dealing with life issues for parents and teens, and writes a blog at keytolifeblog.com.

She is the founder and president of Christian Resource Network, Inc., a non-profit organization providing support to youth and families at christianresourcenetwork.org.

She and her husband, Carl, live in the Boston area, and are the parents of two sons and two daughters and have several grandchildren.

Books Written by the Author:

Standing on His Promises:
Finding Comfort, Hope, and Purpose in the Midst of Your Storm

Prayer and Medication:
Finding Comfort, Hope, and Purpose in the Midst of Your Storm

Prayer and Meditation for Teens:
Finding Comfort, Hope, and Purpose in the Midst of Your Storm

Prayer and Meditation:
Biblical Self-Help Tools for Parents of Teens when You Do Not Know where to Turn

Rise Up:
How to Overcome Your Battles Utilizing Faith and Belief in God

Gentle Breeze:
Finding Comfort, Hope, and Purpose in the Midst of Your Storm

---

Contact us! We'd love to hear from you:

WEB   keytolifepublishingcompany.com
EMAIL admin@keytolifepublishingcompany.com

KEY TO LIFE PUBLISHING COMPANY
P.O. Box 190971 • Boston, MA 02119

  Like us on Facebook:
Facebook.com/keytolifepublishingcompany

Photo Credits

Page 3 © FOYN | Unsplash
Page 5 © Scott Payne | Pixabay
Page 7 © Noppakun Wiropart | 123rf.com
Page 9 © Ian Stewart | Unsplash
Page 11 © Dmitry Kushch | 123rf.com
Page 13 © Gary Bendig | Unsplash
Page 15 © Veniamin Kraskov | 123rf.com
Page 17 Public Domain
Page 19 © Denis Degioanni | Unsplash
Page 21 © Felipe Correia | Unsplash
Page 23 © Kwanchai Lerttanapunyaporn | 123rf.com
Page 25 © David Mark | Pixabay
Page 27 © Art derived from Ashok Munde | Unsplash
Page 29 © Nattachai Sesaud | Stocklib
Page 31 © MH | Teknigram.com
Page 33 © Andreas Lischka | Pixabay3
Page 35 Public Domain, Wikimedia
Page 37 © Plush Design Studio | Unsplash
Page 39 © Quino Al | Unsplash
Page 41 © Photo Adarsh Kummur | Unsplash, modified by MH | Tek
Page 43 Public Domain
Page 46 © Steven Van Loy | Unsplash
Page 47 © Aziz Acharki | Unsplash
Page 49 Found / Modified by MH | Teknigram.com
Page 51 © Liane Metzler | Unsplash
Page 53 © Elias Sch | Pixabay
Page 55 © MH | Teknigram.com
Page 57 © KRiemer | Pixabay
Page 59 © MH | Teknigram.com
Page 61 © **Ashish Thakur | Unsplash**

www.ingramcontent.com/pod-product-compliance
Lightning Source LLC
Chambersburg PA
CBHW020627300426
44112CB00010B/1228